Turbulent Planet

Heat Hazard

Droughts

Claire Watts

Sch

D0313824

www.raintreepublishers.co.uk

Visit our website to find out more information about **Raintree** books.

To order:
☎ Phone 44 (0) 1865 888113
▤ Send a fax to 44 (0) 1865 314091
▢ Visit the Raintree Bookshop at **www.raintreepublishers.co.uk** to browse our catalogue and order online.

First published in Great Britain by Raintree, Halley Court, Jordan Hill, Oxford OX2 8EJ, part of Harcourt Education. Raintree is a registered trademark of Harcourt Education Ltd.

Produced for Raintree by Discovery Books Ltd.

Editorial: Saskia Besier, Melanie Copland and Carol Usher
Design: Michelle Lisseter and Rob Norridge
Illustrations: Peter Bull and Stefan Chabluk
Picture Research: Rachel Tisdale
Consultant: Keith Lye
Production: Duncan Gilbert
Printed and bound in China by South China Printing Company
Originated by Ambassador Litho Ltd

ISBN 1 844 43626 8 (hardback)
08 07 06 05 04
10 9 8 7 6 5 4 3 2 1

ISBN 1 844 43632 2 (paperback)
09 08 07 06 05
10 9 8 7 6 5 4 3 2 1

British Library Cataloguing in Publication Data
Watts, Claire
Heat Hazard : droughts – (Turbulent planet)
1. Drought – Juvenile literature 2. Natural disasters – Juvenile literature
551.5'773

A full catalogue record for this book is available from the British Library.

Photo acknowledgements
p.**4/5**, Corbis/Ecoscene/Rosemary Greenwood; p.**5** top, Corbis/Gary Braasch; p.**5** middle, Corbis/Peter Turnley; p.**5** bottom, Corbis/Gallo Images/Anthony Bannister; p.**6/7**, Corbis/Barnabas Bosshart Science; p.**7**, Corbis/Roger Tidman; p.**8**, Corbis/Chris Rainier; p.**8** left, Corbis Sygma/Patrick Durand; p.**9**, Corbis; p.**10/11**, Corbis/Hulton-Deutsch Collection; p.**10**, Corbis/Gilles Fonlupt p.**11**, Still Pictures/Jim Wark; p.**12/13**, Corbis/Gallo Images/Philip Richardson; p.**13**, Corbis/Liba Taylor; p.**14**, Corbis/Gary Braasch; p.**14** left, Corbis/Gustavo Gilbert; p.**15**, Corbis/Yann Arthus-Bertrand; p.**16/17**, Corbis/Penny Tweedie; p.**16**, Corbis/Ricardo Azoury; p.**18/19**, Corbis/Bettmann; p.**18**, Corbis/Yves Forestier; p.**19**, Science Photo Library/ George Bernard p.**20/21**, Still Pictures/UNEP/Voltchev; p.**20**, NHPA/Daniel Heuclin; p.**21**, Corbis/Charles & Josette Lenars; p.**22/23**, Corbis/Peter Turnley; p.**23**, Science Photo Library/Vanessa Vick; p.**24**, Corbis; p.**24** left, Corbis/ Gilles Fonlupt; p.**25**, Corbis; p.**26**, Corbis/Peter Turnley; p.**26** left, Corbis/Caroline Penn; p.**27**, Still Pictures/Mark Edwards; p.**28**, Corbis/David Reed; p.**29**, Corbis/Charles Krebbs; p.**30/31**, Corbis/Vittoriano Rastelli; p.**30**, Science Photo Library/University of Cambridge Collection of Aerial Photographs; p.**32/33**, Still Pictures/Christian Aid/G Griffiths; p.**33**, Still Pictures/Mark Lynas; p.**34**, Corbis; p.**35**, Corbis/ Craig Aurness; p.**35** right, Science Photo Library/Novosti Press Agency; p.**36/37**, Corbis/Keren Su; p.**36**, Corbis/Lester Lefkowitz; p.**37**, Science Photo Library/David Parker; p.**38/39**, Corbis/Gallo Images/Anthony Bannister; p.**38**, Corbis/Richard T Nowitz; p.**39**, Corbis/ George D Lepp; p.**40/41**, Corbis/Jeremy Horner; p.**40**, Corbis; p.**42/43**, Chromosohm/Joseph Sohm; p.**42**, Corbis/Yann Arthus-Bertrand; p.**43**, Discovery Picture Library; p.**44**, Corbis/ Ecoscene/Rosemary Greenwood; p.**45**, Corbis.

Cover photograph reproduced with permission of Getty Images/Brand X

Contents

Any words appearing in the text in bold, **like this**, are explained in the Glossary. You can also look out for them in the Disaster words box at the bottom of each page.

Dry as dust

Hot, dry winds sweep across the land. They carry a cloud of dusty soil. The air is filled with the choking dust. Here and there, drooping plants struggle to live in the cracked earth. No water flows in the wide riverbed.

The people watch in despair. Their crops are failing. Their **livestock** weaken and die. Slowly but surely, the people begin to **starve**.

No rain

What terrible disaster has happened? No great storm or war has caused this destruction. There is simply no rain. When rain does not fall for a long time, rivers, lakes and streams dry up and plants die. A drought begins.

With no crops, no water and no money, the people start to leave their homes. After months of near-starvation they are weak. Even so, they travel vast distances across the countryside in search of food and water. They may never return to their homes.

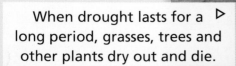

When drought lasts for a ▷ long period, grasses, trees and other plants dry out and die.

barren   where nothing will grow
fertile   capable of growing plants

Barren land

Severe drought can leave the land ruined and **barren**. Even when rain begins to fall, the water washes away the dusty soil. With careful farming, the soil may become **fertile** once more. Plants may gradually start to grow on the land again. However, some land never recovers from drought.

Find out later...

How can people cause droughts?

What happens when there is a drought?

What can people do to prevent drought?

livestock   farm animals
starve   have little or no food

What is a drought?

Some areas of the world are dry all the time. In these places rain almost never falls. These are the world's deserts.

Waiting for rain

Places struck by drought are not the same as deserts. Droughts happen all over the world, in places where people expect rain to fall. In some places, it is normal to have a long season of dry weather followed by a season of heavy rain. But, sometimes the rain comes too late, not enough rain falls or no rain comes at all. This is when the crops begin to die and the **water sources** dry up. This is the start of a drought.

A drought may last a month, or several years. There may be some rain, but not as much as the people, animals and plants need.

Drought profile – Bolivia 1983

In 1983 drought struck Bolivia in South America and 80 per cent of the normal autumn harvest was lost. The people in the countryside suffered, but they were not the only ones. In the city of Potosi, none of the 104,000 people had any water.

This is an aerial view of the △ town of Cochabamba, Bolivia. The photo shows the dry, dusty ground during a drought.

How much rain?

It is hard to say exactly how little rain makes a drought. It depends on where you are. In a hot, dry country like Libya in Africa, people do not expect much rain. Less than 180 millimetres in a year is a drought in Libya. The island of Bali in Indonesia normally gets 1.7 metres of rain in a year. There it usually rains every day, all year round. In Bali, one week without rain could be called a drought.

True or false?

Droughts only happen in hot places.

Answer: False.

Drought occurs when the amount of water is far below normal. This can happen in cold and snowy areas as well as hot ones.

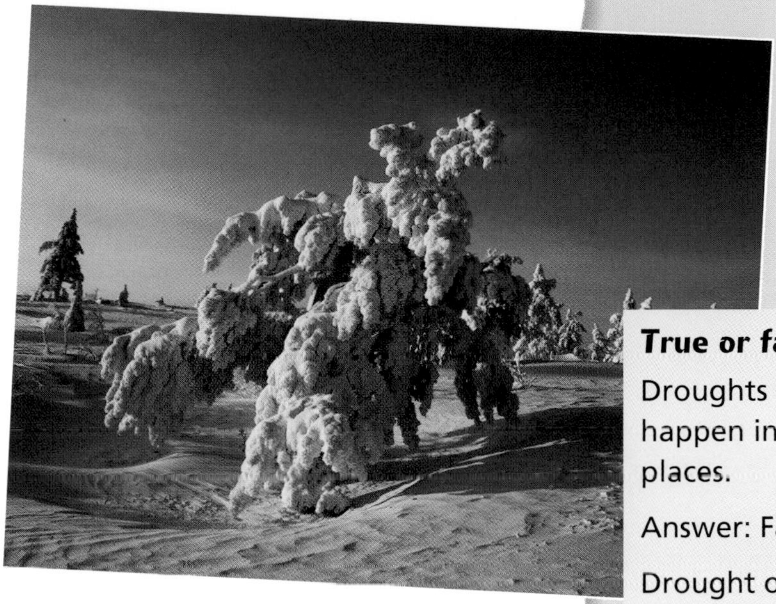

This map shows the parts of the world regularly affected by droughts and the places mentioned in this book. ▽

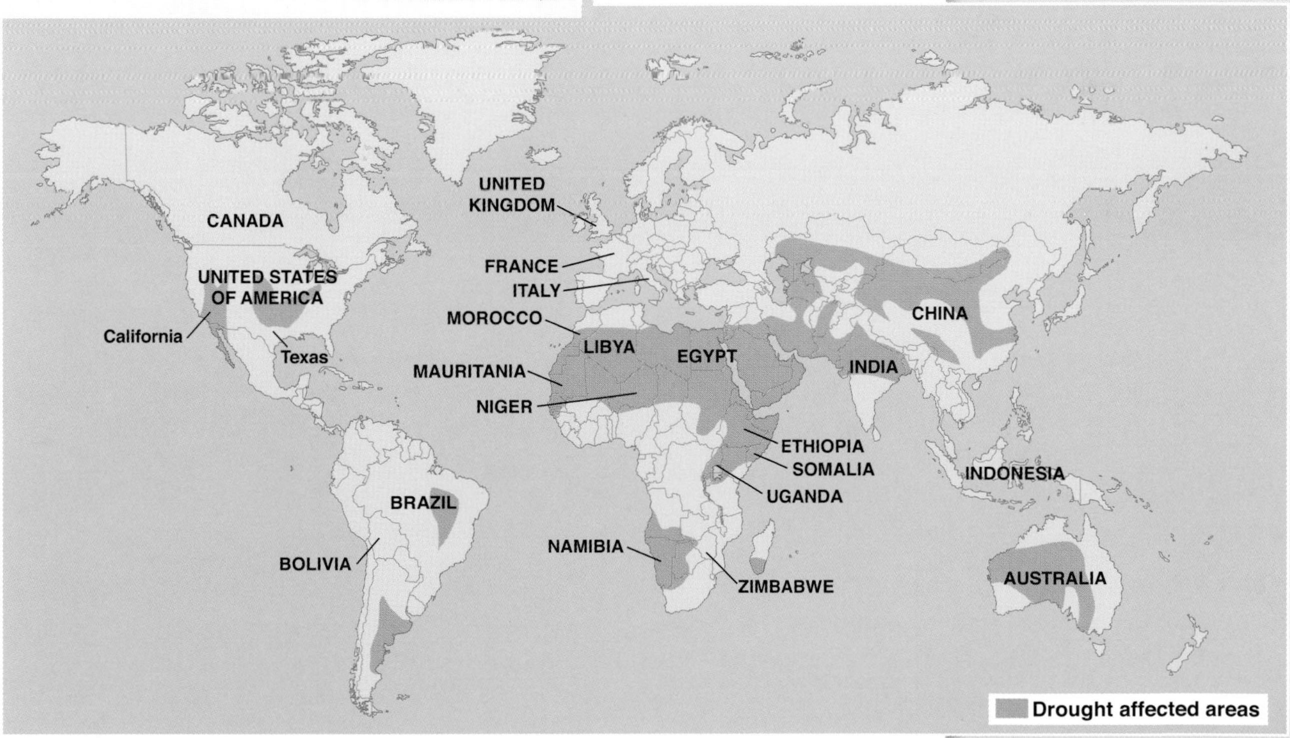

CANADA
UNITED STATES OF AMERICA
California
Texas
UNITED KINGDOM
FRANCE
ITALY
MOROCCO
LIBYA
EGYPT
MAURITANIA
NIGER
CHINA
INDIA
ETHIOPIA
SOMALIA
UGANDA
INDONESIA
BRAZIL
BOLIVIA
NAMIBIA
ZIMBABWE
AUSTRALIA
Drought affected areas

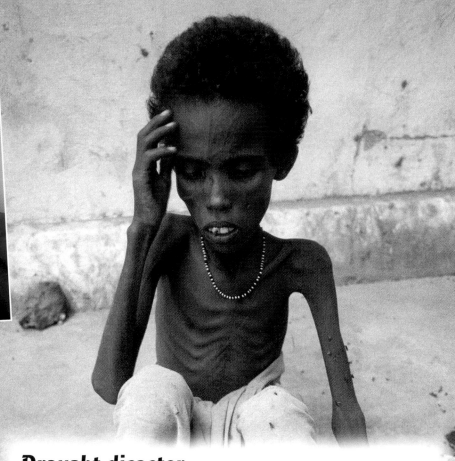

The secret drought

The Ethiopian President, Colonel Haile Mariam Mengistu, and his government tried to keep the 1984 drought secret from the rest of the world. This was probably because the government bought weapons instead of food for its people. People were already dying when **aid organizations** arrived there.

Drought disaster

When we think of droughts, one country above all the others comes to mind: Ethiopia. Ethiopia has suffered from droughts over the past twenty years. Some years, the rains do come. The crops grow and people lead normal lives. In other years, drought strikes.

Drought hit Ethiopia from 1984 to 1985. This was one of the worst droughts ever. Eight million people did not have enough food and one million people died.

Ethiopia's periods of drought are happening more often. When the rains finally do come there is no time for the land to recover before the next drought starts.

People all around the world were shocked when they saw the pictures of starving Ethiopians on TV. ▷

aid organization group that helps people in need, usually in developing countries

Why Ethiopia?

Why does drought cause so many problems in Ethiopia? Most of Ethiopia's people work on the land. They grow crops to feed their families. If they grow any extra crops, they sell them to buy other things they need. If the rains do not come, the crops do not grow, so the people have no food. They also have no money to buy food or anything else.

Ethiopia is a **developing country**. There is not enough money to help people cope with drought. The government cannot afford to provide them with food and water when drought comes. Each time a severe drought strikes Ethiopia, the government has to rely on help from other countries to feed the **starving** people.

July 13, 1985

THE GREATEST SHOW ON EARTH

Across the world today, people turned on their TVs to see Live Aid. This is one of the biggest pop concerts ever held. The concert raised £70 million for the starving people of Ethiopia. This is the largest amount of money a single event has ever made for **charity**.

developing country   poor country that is trying to become richer and improve its living conditions, like Ethiopia and Somalia in Africa

Short of water

People who live in hot countries on the edge of deserts expect drought to happen sometimes. In the cooler areas of the world, such as north-west Europe, drought is more unexpected. These countries usually have between 50 and 100 millimetres of rain every month. In 1976, north-west Europe suffered a severe drought. The problems started in 1975. The summer was very hot and there was little rain. Most of the water in the **reservoirs** was used up. There was not enough rain the next winter to refill the reservoirs. Early in 1976, people realized that the water was running out.

This reservoir in Northamptonshire, UK fell to over 6 metres (20 feet) below its normal level during the 1976 drought. ▽

When grass dries up like this, cows cannot get any ◁ nourishment from it.

developed country   rich country with modern living conditions, such as Australia, Britain and the USA

Water queues

In 1976, less than half the normal amount of rain fell in north-west Europe. By August, only one-quarter of the water in the reservoirs was left. In some places, water to people's homes was cut off. People lined up to fetch water from taps in the streets. These taps are called **standpipes**. Crops shrivelled in the fields. Rivers, lakes and ponds dried up. Fish and other creatures died.

Coping with drought

Wealthy **developed countries**, like those in north-west Europe, can cope with a drought more easily than poor **developing countries**. If the harvest is affected by drought for one year, people will not starve. There is plenty of stored food for them to eat. They have the money to buy in food from other countries.

Drought profile – California

California, in the USA, suffers badly from droughts. In southern California, people built cities and created farmland in desert. Water is piped in from other areas or pumped up from underground.

The Owens River near Bishop, California has dried up completely. ▷

reservoir   man-made or natural lake or large tank for storing water
standpipe   upright water pipe with a tap on it

Why droughts happen

Water cycle

All the water on the Earth is used again and again. Sunlight warms up the Earth. Water from the oceans, the ground and plants evaporates into the air as invisible **water vapour**. The water vapour rises into the sky. As the air cools. the vapour forms water droplets. This is called **condensation**. The water droplets collect into clouds. When the clouds become big enough, the water falls as rain or snow.

In most places, most of the time, there is a balance between the amount of rain and the amount of water used. In a drought, this balance is upset by changes in the normal weather patterns.

Not a breath of wind

All over the Earth, the air presses down. This is called air **pressure**. Changes in air pressure cause different types of weather. Low pressure brings wet, cloudy, changeable weather. If an area of high pressure settles over an area, the weather is usually calm and very hot in summer or calm and cold in winter. No winds blow clouds into the area. Dry weather may last for weeks.

Disaster words   condensation   droplets of water formed from water vapour when air cools
evaporate   change from liquid water into invisible water vapour

Disappearing into the air

In hot weather, thousands of litres of water **evaporate** from rivers, lakes and oceans into the air every day. Even if rain falls, when the weather is extremely hot, it may evaporate before it reaches the ground.

Dried up

Water evaporates from the leaves of plants into the air too. This is called **transpiration**. In hot, dry weather, plants lose water more quickly. They then take more water up from the soil through their roots. This makes up for the water they are losing, but it also dries out the soil. When less rain falls, and more water is lost through evaporation and transpiration, a drought can follow. It does not take much to upset the balance.

Water stored in a metal storage tank with a lid cannot evaporate in the hot sun.
▽

transpiration   way plants lose water from their leaves through evaporation
water vapour   water in the form of an invisible gas in the air

Traditional ways – slash and burn agriculture

Many **rainforest** people clear small areas of forest to plant crops. They cut trees down and burn the wood. When the land is first cleared the soil is very fertile. They farm this land for about three years and then move on. The patch is left and slowly becomes overgrown. Gradually the forest returns.

A man-made problem

People can bring about droughts too. Sometimes, it is because people use too much water and not enough rain falls to replace it. Other times, droughts happen because people have changed the natural landscape.

Dusty soil

The first thing to be affected by the lack of water is the soil. If the soil is **fertile**, it stores enough water to last a few weeks without rain. When the soil is poor, water **evaporates** from it quickly. After a few days without rain, plants begin to wilt. Poor soil cracks and turns to dust very easily.

When trees are cut down from a hillside, the soil left behind dries out and can slip down the hillside. ▷

atmosphere   layer of gases that surround the Earth
condense   when a gas turns into a liquid

If farmers grow the same crops again and again in the same area, the plants use up all the **nutrients** in the soil. Too many animals, grazing on the same piece of land for a long time, can also ruin the soil. Then the soil becomes poor and drought affects it more easily.

Felling the trees

Trees protect the soil. Leaves from the trees shade the soil and reduce evaporation. Fallen leaves rot and put nutrients back into the soil. Tree roots hold the soil together. This helps the soil hold on to water and stops **erosion**. But trees are often cut down to clear land for farming, building or for wood. When this happens, the soil no longer stores water and dries out easily.

Trees make rain

Forests release huge amounts of **water vapour** into the **atmosphere** when they **transpire**. The water vapour **condenses** to form clouds. This returns water to the Earth as rain. When the trees are cut down, there is less transpiration, and so less rain falls.

△ Trees once filled this landscape. Huge areas of forest are cut down all over the world every year to grow crops, build houses or create cattle ranches.

erosion wearing away by action of wind and water
nutrient substance needed for growth

When drought strikes

Water and disease

When water supplies run out, people have to drink any water they can find. They may take water from puddles when it rains or from a river **polluted** with **sewage**. Dirty drinking water can lead to outbreaks of disease.

Very little rain has fallen, but nothing drastic has happened yet. The water levels of the rivers and lakes still seem fine, but the water in the soil is drying out. Plants keep losing water through their leaves by **transpiration**. They cannot take in enough water to make up for what is lost. They stop growing and begin to **wilt**. Wilting crops in the fields are the first sign of a drought.

Water runs out

People carry on using water normally as the dry period continues. The water continues to **evaporate** from **water sources**. Gradually, water supplies start to dry up. People cannot water their crops. The crops die. Soon there is no water for drinking or for washing.

When water is scarce, people may have to use dirty water ◁ for washing and cooking.

Disaster words   mineral salt   salts found in the soil
pollution   presence of high levels of harmful substances

Wearing away the land

If the drought continues, the ground becomes dry and cracked. It cannot hold on to any moisture. The dusty soil is worn away by the wind. **Barren** patches of land are left behind. Once the drought is over, heavy rain may wash away the remaining soil. This action of wind and rain is called **erosion**.

Poisoned earth

When a drought goes on for several years, the land is no longer fertile. High quantities of **mineral salts** build up in the soil if there is no rain to wash them away. These poison the soil and make it impossible for plants to grow there, even when it does rain.

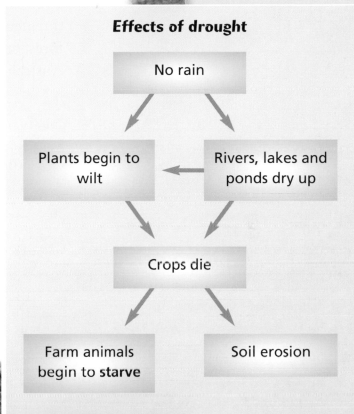

Effects of drought

No rain

Plants begin to wilt ← Rivers, lakes and ponds dry up

Crops die

Farm animals begin to **starve**   Soil erosion

When drought strikes, **livestock** will die unless farmers can provide a constant source of food and water.

---

sewage   waste water produced by humans
wilt   when plants droop because of lack of water

Fire and dust

At the height of the drought the **vegetation** is bone-dry. Lightning or even a dropped match can set the countryside on fire. Fire can spread through **undergrowth** at over 140 kilometres (88 miles) per hour. This threatens human and animal lives. Huge areas of forest and bush fires burn every year in parts of Australia, the USA and southern France.

Swirling dust

Winds blowing across the dried-out landscape whip the soil into a swirling **dust storm**. A cloud of hot dust fills the air. It shuts out the light. Because there is no vegetation to hold down the soil, loose **topsoil** blows hundreds of kilometres.

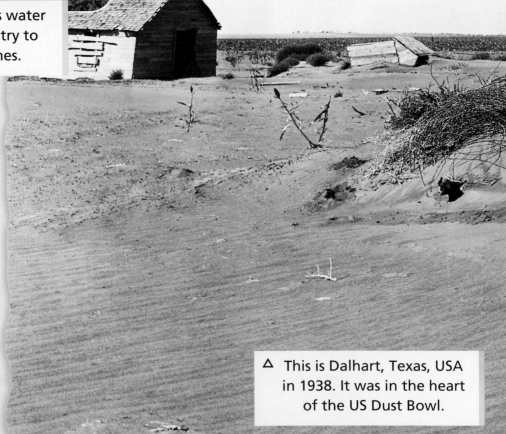

△ A helicopter dumps water on a forest fire to try to control the flames.

Amazing but true

Australia's lodge-pole and jack pine trees need bush-fires to **reproduce**. The cones of these trees have to be burned in a fire before they will open to release their seeds.

△ This is Dalhart, Texas, USA in 1938. It was in the heart of the US Dust Bowl.

dust storm   cloud of dust blown by the wind
reproduce   make offspring or members of the same species

Dust Bowl

From 1931 to 1938 a major drought brought dust storms to the USA's Great Plains. The crisis stretched over a huge area from Texas in the south to the borders of Canada in the north. People called this part of the USA 'The Dust Bowl'.

Farming was the problem

Americans moved west and arrived on the Great Plains in the nineteenth century. They ploughed up the natural grassland to plant wheat. Grass has long roots. These bind the soil together. Wheat, on the other hand, has short roots. Wheat was grown for many years. The soil became less and less **fertile**. When drought set in, the crops failed and fierce storms blew away the topsoil. Thousands of farmers left their farms because their land was useless.

The Great Fire of London

One of the most famous fires followed months of drought. In the summer of 1666, London's wooden houses were as dry as firewood. The water level in the River Thames was very low. The fire started on September 2 and destroyed 13,000 buildings.

undergrowth plants that grow beneath trees in a forest
vegetation all the plants that grow in an area

The spreading desert

When droughts go on month after month, the bare, dusty ground reflects back more of the sun's heat. The reflected heat stops clouds forming and no rain falls. Gradually a larger and larger area dries out. If the drought continues for long enough, the area will never recover. It will turn into desert.

Thirty-year drought

Areas on the edge of deserts are more likely to become deserts too. South of Africa's Sahara desert lies the Sahel region. For the past thirty years, this area has suffered from drought.

The Sahel usually receives between 250 and 500 millimetres of rain each year. This is enough rain to allow grasses to grow. **Traditionally**, the people of the Sahel grazed herds of sheep and goats on the grasslands.

Where is the Sahel?

Areas like the Sahel lie next to deserts. They are very prone to drought. Sometimes, if the rains fail for long enough they turn into deserts too.

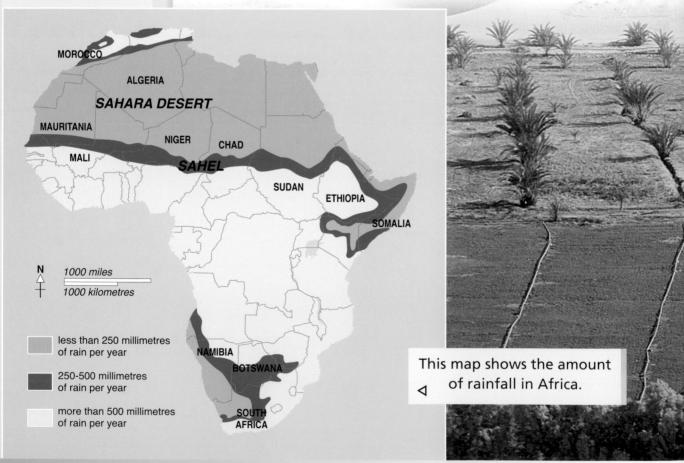

This map shows the amount of rainfall in Africa.

Map labels:
MOROCCO
ALGERIA
SAHARA DESERT
MAURITANIA
NIGER
CHAD
MALI
SAHEL
SUDAN
ETHIOPIA
SOMALIA
NAMIBIA
BOTSWANA
SOUTH AFRICA

N
1000 miles
1000 kilometres

less than 250 millimetres of rain per year

250-500 millimetres of rain per year

more than 500 millimetres of rain per year

Disaster words fertility ability to grow things
nomadic moving from place to place

Many mouths to feed

In recent years, the number of people has grown. This has made things worse. To feed the people, farmers have started to keep more animals. They have planted crops on the same land, year after year. The land has been over-used and the soil has gradually lost its **fertility**. Each time drought strikes the Sahel, more of the poor soil is removed. Gradually the region is turning into **barren** desert, where nothing will grow.

This picture shows just how close the rolling sand-dunes of the desert are to the fertile lands in the Sahel region. ▽

△ Tuareg people drawing water from a well for their cattle.

traditional   way of life passed down from generation to generation

Famine

**To: Peter
From: Helga,
Red Cross Camp,
Somalia**

The countryside is covered with dead animals. I just hope we've got here in time to save the children. You should see them, they just sit so still and silent. No one plays – they're too weak.

Month follows month with no sign of rain. The crisis deepens. Food supplies begin to run out. The grass dries out and dies. Other animal **fodder** is used up. The cows become thin and stop producing milk. People are forced to kill and eat their **livestock**.

Feeding the hungry

With no crops and no livestock, the people have no food left to eat. They have nothing left to sell. There is no money to buy food either. Emergency supplies of food must reach the region before the people **starve**.

Famine is a common event in Africa and Asia. It is not only caused by drought. Disease or storms can wipe out crops and leave people starving.

diet   amount and type of food eaten
disability   injury or disease that prevents a person doing something

◁ Somali people line up for food.

Starving children

Children under five suffer from the effects of starvation first. Without proper food, children's limbs become thin. Their stomachs swell up and they stop growing. They catch diseases more easily. They may grow up with mental or physical **disabilities**. This is because their poor **diet** stopped them from developing properly.

An on-going problem

The problem of famine often continues after the drought has ended. During the famine, farmers and their families might eat all their seed because there is no other food. If they do this, there is nothing to plant for next year's crop.

Even if they do have seeds, the farmers could be too weak to work on the land. They may have even left their farms altogether to search for food. If farmers do not plant crops, there will certainly be no harvest. The famine will continue.

famine going without food for a long time
fodder animal feed

Abandoning the land

When people in **developing countries** begin to **starve**, they do not wait around for food and water to arrive. They pack their things and leave their homes. Most people do not own houses or land and this makes it easier for them to leave. When a lot of people leave an area, it is called **migration**. Some people travel hundreds of kilometres to **refugee camps** where there is food. Sometimes they take their herds of animals with them. They hope to find empty land for the animals to graze. Other people migrate to cities to find jobs.

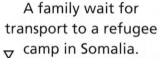

A family wait for transport to a refugee camp in Somalia. ▽

True or false?

Drought is always bad for all farmers.

Answer: False.

When a drought destroys most of the crops and **livestock**, farmers who do manage to produce some crops and livestock will get a very high price for their goods.

insurance   agreement to provide money in case of a disaster
migration   moving from one place to settle in another

Government aid

Migrating people cannot grow any food. They have to rely on governments or **aid organizations** to feed them. Drought hits developing countries, such as Ethiopia, very hard. There is no money to pay for schools and hospitals if it is all used for **famine** relief.

Drought insurance

When drought hits a **developed country**, such as Australia, the disaster is not so bad. Developed countries have stores of food and water for the people to rely on. Most farmers would not leave their farms after just one year of drought. Farmers and businesses have **insurance**. This helps them to survive even when they lose one year's crops or products. The government has enough money to help out when things get very serious.

Drought profile – Mauritania in north-west Africa

Long-term drought can completely change a country. Before the 1968 drought, two-thirds of Mauritania's people lived as **nomads**. They kept animals on the land. When the drought struck, it was impossible for so many animals to find food and water. By 1976 only one-third of the people were nomads, the rest had migrated to the cities to find jobs.

This picture shows the dry, dusty landscape left after ◁ Mauritania's drought.

refugee camp   place where migrating people gather to receive aid

After the drought

A huge city of tents and huts stretches as far as the eye can see. This is a **refugee camp** in a **developing country**. The first **priority** in a drought is to give food and water to as many people as possible. Huge refugee camps are often set up. All the people from the surrounding area can gather in one spot to receive food.

Drought profile – Uganda 1999

When drought struck the north and east of Uganda in 1999, the government acted quickly. Food was transported from the south and west of the country, where there was plenty. The hungry people had enough food to last until the drought was over. This swift action meant there was no **famine** or **migration**.

△ This is a refugee camp in Somalia. There are tents far into the distance.

A Ugandan woman scoops △ water from a muddy puddle.

Disaster words charity organization that helps those in need
NGO non-governmental organization, also called an aid organization

Helpless and hungry

Large refugee camps create problems of their own. People in refugee camps have no way of looking after themselves. It is not just a matter of giving people food and water. Everything has to be provided: shelter, medicine and clothing.

It is better if **aid organizations** take food and water to where the people live. If people have enough food and water at home, they will not have to leave their lands.

Helping people in need

Who are aid workers? Sometimes they are people sent by the country's government to help in the crisis. More often, they belong to international aid organizations, such as the Red Cross or Oxfam. These organizations are **charities**. They were set up to help people in need throughout the world. They are not connected to the governments of any particular country. These charities are often known as non-governmental organizations or **NGOs**.

Drought relief priorities

1. Hand out food and water
2. Hand out fodder
3. Provide constant water supplies
4. Hand out seeds for new crops

The US government has given these sacks of wheat to help feed the drought-stricken people of Ethiopia.

Effects of rainfall on land struck by drought

Rain falls

Soil water recovers

Reservoirs, lakes and rivers recover

Groundwater recovers

Water for life

When the rain starts to fall at last, the water soaks into the soil. The land may quickly recover from drought as long as it is not washed away by floods or blown away by the wind. Farmers can plant the crops straight away. Hopefully these crops will provide food for the next year.

Next, the rain begins to refill rivers, lakes and streams. Sometimes a lot of very heavy rain falls at the end of a drought. Too much rain brings a new crisis. Rivers can burst their banks and flood the surrounding land.

A girl digs for water in a dried up riverbed in Zimbabwe. ▷

Disaster words   germinate   start to grow
groundwater   water stored beneath the soil

Underground water

Beneath the soil there are hard layers of rock. Water can seep through some rocks and collect in them. This is called **groundwater**. Even when a drought has left the soil dusty and the rivers are dried up, groundwater can usually still be found.

During the worst of the drought, people may find groundwater by digging at the lowest point of a dried-up riverbed. Wells dug deep into the rock will usually provide groundwater long after other **water sources** have dried up. If a pump is added to the well, the water can be used to **irrigate** farming land in times of drought.

There is a problem with relying on groundwater. It is impossible to tell how much is left. Groundwater is the last water source to be affected by a drought. However, when it runs out, it takes a very long time to refill.

Desert flowers

You should visit a dry area just after rain has fallen. Then you will see how quickly soil recovers from drought. Before the rain, the ground is **barren** and looks as if nothing will ever grow there. After the rain, tiny seeds **germinate** and the desert is covered with flowers.

irrigate water crops

Predicting droughts

Can we work out when a drought is going to happen, before it actually does? **Meteorologists** do not think so. Droughts are difficult to **forecast**. They happen very gradually. Meteorologists would have to forecast the weather for about six months ahead. Meteorologists cannot do this accurately over a long period of time.

Waiting

Droughts seem to happen in a regular pattern. The patterns can give meteorologists an idea of when to start looking out for signs of drought. But meteorologists cannot tell exactly when a drought will happen from this information.

True or false?

Satellites can be used to predict droughts.

Answer: True.

Photographs from satellites show failing crops, long before any other signs of drought are noticeable.

△ On this **infrared** picture taken from the air, healthy crops appear deep pink. Failed crops appear patchy pink and white.

forecast   give information about something that might happen
meteorologist   person who studies and reports on the weather

Watching

Monitoring the land for drought is not difficult. Anyone can be trained to look out for signs. The first sign is usually changes in the **vegetation**. Plants may be small, **wilted** or simply not as green as usual for the time of year. There could be a dry period at an odd time of year or an increase in wind or **dust storms**. Water levels might be lower. More animals might die.

Scientists can gather information about the earliest signs of drought. If people spot these early warnings, they can take action and reduce the effect of the drought.

India, June 12th

Dear Ravi
The rains started at last, but I don't think enough rain is falling. By now the fields should be flooded so the rice can grow properly. Instead you can see the bare soil. Looks like we are headed for a drought.

◁ An Italian farmer inspects his orange crop for signs of drought.

monitor watch carefully
satellite object in space used to observe our planet

El Niño

In some regions of the world, predicting droughts is not too difficult. These droughts are caused by a weather pattern called **El Niño**. El Niño creates some of the most extreme weather on the planet. When El Niño appeared in 1982 and 1983 it caused weather disasters across a quarter of the world. There were **dust storms** and bush fires in Australia and drought in South-East Asia.

Drought and floods

So what is El Niño? El Niño is a change in the flow of ocean **currents** in the central Pacific Ocean. These changes affect normal rainfall patterns all over the world.

El Niño

In most years, the winds and surface currents of the Pacific Ocean flow westwards. These carry warm water away from South America. El Niño occurs when these winds and currents change direction. The warm waters push closer than normal against the coasts of North and South America.

This diagram explains how El Niño happens.
▽

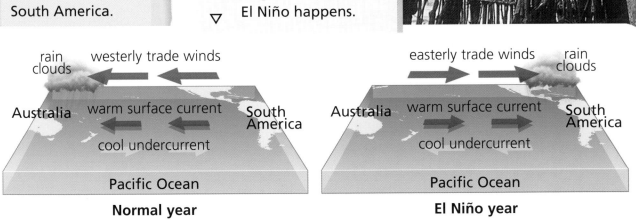

Normal year	El Niño year
rain clouds — westerly trade winds	easterly trade winds — rain clouds
Australia — warm surface current — South America	Australia — warm surface current — South America
cool undercurrent	cool undercurrent
Pacific Ocean	Pacific Ocean

The floods in this Kenyan ▷ village can be traced back to the El Niño weather system.

Disaster words   current   steady flow of water or air in one direction
drought-resistant   able to grow even in drought conditions

The 1997 to 1998 El Niño caused very high rainfall in East Africa, giving it a bumper coffee harvest. Meanwhile, in South America, Brazil suffered drought. Its coffee crop was a failure. At the same time central Asia, the north-west USA and Canada had heat waves, while countries in central Europe were flooded.

Early warning

By studying the ocean's currents, scientists may soon be able to predict when El Niño will arrive. They would then be able to **forecast** extreme weather events connected with El Niño, up to a year in advance. If an area is likely to be affected by drought, the people will be able to prepare. They can stock up on water and plant **drought-resistant** crops.

Did you know?

El Niño is Spanish for 'Christ child'. El Niño gets its name because it usually starts around Christmas. This is when Christians celebrate the birth of Jesus Christ.

△ This dust storm in China has brought traffic to a standstill.

El Niño pattern of wind and ocean currents that brings extreme weather

Fighting drought

Drought does not have to be a serious problem. When the first signs of a water shortage appear, people should reduce the amount of water they use. This is an important way to fight drought. In some places people could be banned from using garden hoses and sprinklers.

Every drop counts

Once a drought has begun, water has to be **rationed** carefully. This protects supplies. When sharing out water, it is important to look at the needs of everyone. First, people need drinking water. Then water must be set apart for animals to drink, for washing and for watering crops.

Although we cannot change the weather, we can reduce the worst effects of drought. Scientists and governments can help improve how people farm the land and use water.

Traditional ways – rain dances

The Hopi people of the south-western USA perform **traditional** rain dances. In this way they ask the spirits to bring rain to their hot, dry lands.

Disaster words   cloud-seeding   putting chemicals into clouds to make rain
dam   barrier built across a river or stream to stop the water flowing

This man is digging a well in Morocco. He will hopefully tap into water beneath the ground. ▽

Making rain

Scientists have tried to make rain. They have dropped chemicals into clouds from aircraft, like the one shown below. This is supposed to make water drops freeze faster and make rain fall. It is called **cloud-seeding**. It is hard to tell if cloud-seeding really brings rain or if the rain would have happened anyway.

At-risk areas

The first step is to work out where in the world drought might happen. These areas are easy to identify. They have usually been hit by drought before. Next, these areas should make sure they have a reliable, constant supply of water. They could tap into **groundwater** by digging a well or build a **dam**. Then farmers have to learn new farming methods. These methods could stop drought ruining their land.

ration share out fairly

23 October 2000

China to divert river

The Chinese government has announced a plan to divert the Yangtze River 3000 kilometres (1775 miles) to the north of the country. This area often gets droughts. The project will cost around US $18 billion.

A constant supply

The key to winning the war against drought is to gather and store as much water as possible. That way, if the rain stops or the **water sources** dry up, there will be water supplies to last a long time.

Dam building

One way to store water is to build **dams** across rivers and streams. The water builds up behind the dam to create a deep lake. The huge Aswan High Dam provides enough water for all the farmland in Egypt, all year. Dams can also be used to generate **hydro-electric power**.

△ The massive Hoover Dam, Nevada, USA. If a dam breaks there would be massive floods in the valleys below.

△ This hilly ground has been terraced for growing rice.

Disaster words hydro-electric power electricity produced by running water
irrigate water crops

Saving the rain

It is not just a matter of storing water. Even building small soil dams around crops can help. These dams stop the rainwater running off the soil. The water soaks into the soil around the plants' roots instead. In hillier places, farmers dig a series of wide flat steps called **terraces** into the hillside. They grow their crops on these. The terraces also help to stop rainwater running straight down the hill. This reduces soil **erosion**.

If farmers cannot rely on the rain, farmers might be able to pump up **groundwater** to **irrigate** their land.

Traditional ways – dowsing for water

Dowsing is an ancient method of finding water under the ground. The dowser walks along holding a forked stick out in front. When the stick drops it is supposed to be above water.

terrace   flat area on a hillside

Looking after the land

Drought makes farming difficult and it can cause long-term damage to the land. The best way to fight drought is to learn how to grow crops using less water. Governments and **aid organizations** help farmers to do this.

A farmworker tends spineless cacti.
▽

Some crops need less water to grow than other crops. Farmers can plant these instead. For example, a crop called sorghum needs less water to grow than maize. Farmers can use sorghum for animal **fodder** and grain just as well as maize. Scientists are also developing **drought-resistant** seeds. These can survive drought and recover once the rains come.

Mexico

Dear Julia

We have been planting cacti in the sand around the edges of the fields – but not the spiny kind! The idea is to anchor down the sand, so it can't blow away if the weather gets very dry. Even better than that, if there's a drought, the cacti can be used to feed the cattle. They can get moisture from them too, when there's hardly any water around. What an amazing crop!

Jean-Pierre

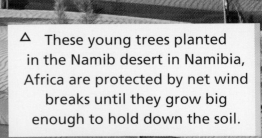

△ These young trees planted in the Namib desert in Namibia, Africa are protected by net wind breaks until they grow big enough to hold down the soil.

Disaster words   drought-resistant   able to survive in drought conditions
fodder   animal feed

Livestock

In dry areas it is easier to rear **livestock** than grow crops. In the driest areas, farmers can use most of their land for rearing animals. In areas where there is more rain, farmers can grow crops.

Animals can strip the ground of **vegetation** and even eat bark off trees. If farmers move their livestock around often, the land has a chance to recover. Farmers can shut their herds up in fields when drought strikes.

Trees

If farmers plant trees or shrubs around their fields, the roots help to anchor the soil. The trees grow into a **wind break**. This stops the fierce winds blowing the dry soil away. Some trees also give food and other crops for farmers to eat or sell.

Traditional ways – animal manure

Animals can graze on the stubble left in the fields after the crops have been harvested. This has two benefits. The animals have another source of food, and the **manure** they leave **fertilizes** the ground for next year's crop.

▽ Sheep graze in a stubble field.

wind break   screen to stop the wind

Climate change

The Earth's **climate** is changing. The balance of gases in the **atmosphere** has altered. **Pollution** from industry, vehicle **exhausts** and other human activities have caused this. There is more heat trapped in the atmosphere now. This has led to a rise in temperatures all over the world. These changes are usually called **global warming**. The rising temperatures are not the only problem.

Climate change may lead to more extreme weather events, such as droughts and floods. Droughts are already becoming more frequent in some places, such as the Sahel region in Africa.

Possible effects of global warming

- Rise in sea level
- Stronger El Niño events
- More droughts at the edges of deserts
- More extreme weather events such as droughts, floods, storms
- Drier zones in the middle of **continents**
- Wetter weather over the oceans
- More autumn and winter rain, less spring and summer rain in certain areas

Low-lying islands like this △ would be lost under the sea if sea levels rise.

△ Traffic jams pump gases into the atmosphere.

atmosphere   layer of gases that surround the Earth
climate   weather patterns over a long period of time

Wetter winters, drier summers

Climate change could also affect the growing seasons of plants in many countries. Rainfall patterns seem to be changing. In some places there is more rain in autumn and winter and less in spring and summer. Many places in the world will need to build **reservoirs** and **irrigation** systems to cope with both floods and droughts.

The changing Earth

People will have to adapt. No one really knows what effect global warming will have. Scientists spend their whole lives studying the Earth's climate and they still cannot give us the answers.

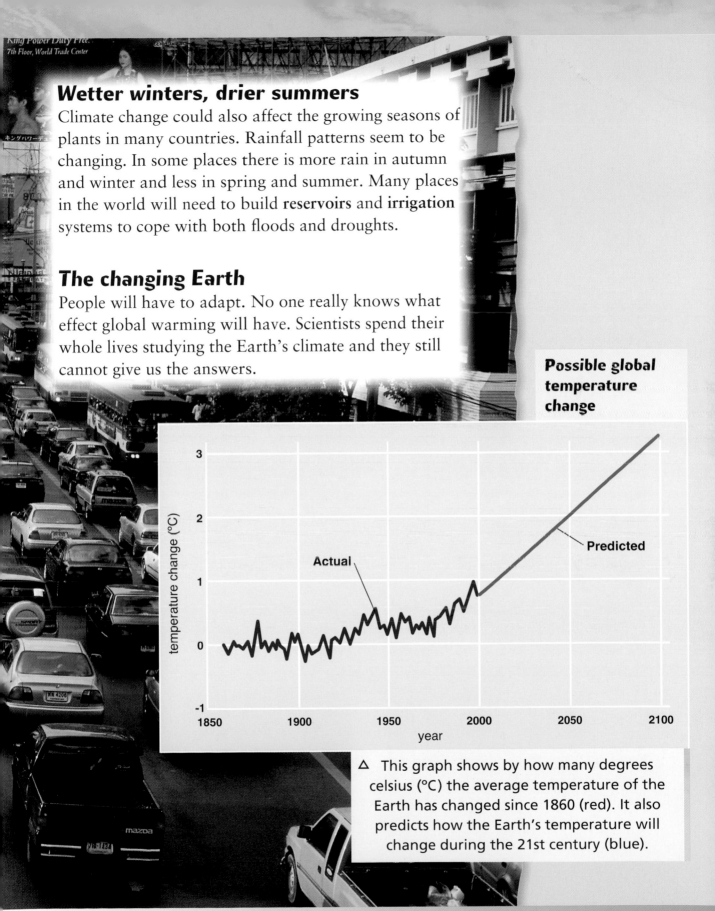

Possible global temperature change

△ This graph shows by how many degrees celsius (°C) the average temperature of the Earth has changed since 1860 (red). It also predicts how the Earth's temperature will change during the 21st century (blue).

global warming way that the Earth's climate is warming up
pollution presence of high levels of harmful substances

Surviving drought

If you ever find yourself in conditions of extreme drought, would you know how to survive? First you should work out how much water you have left and how long it will be until you can get more. Then **ration** your supply carefully to make it last. Try to rest in the shade as much as possible. This will help to save your body's moisture.

Taking it for granted

Most people in **developed countries** will never find themselves in this situation. Droughts do happen, but most have very little effect on ordinary people there.

Tips for water conservation

✓ Never pour water down the drain when there may be another use for it, such as watering plants

✓ Repair dripping taps

✓ Cut down the amount of water needed to fill up the toilet cistern after each flush. Placing something into the tank, like a brick, can do this

✓ Place a bucket in the shower to catch water to give to plants

✓ Take short showers instead of a bath

✓ Do not let the water run when brushing your teeth

◁ Global warming may cause lakes and rivers to dry up, leaving fishing boats like this stranded.

Disaster words   population   total number of people living in a place

When water runs out

With **global warming**, there are likely to be more droughts. **Water sources** may become much less reliable in many places. The world's **population** is growing, so the demand for water will increase too. We must learn not to take water for granted and to save our supplies. Today, most people in developed countries use water as if it will never run out. We leave the water running while we brush our teeth and take baths whenever we want. If we had to live with the threat of drought every day, what a shock we would all have.

Amazing but true
If a tap makes one drip per second, 12,300 litres of water per year is wasted. This would fill more than six Olympic swimming pools.

△ Make sure taps are always turned off properly.

Find out more

Organizations

Weather Channel

This website is run by the USA TV's Weather Channel. It has a weather encyclopedia, plus news, **forecasts** and historical information about weather.

www.weather.com

BBC Weather

Here you will find forecasts, news and features all about the weather.

www.bbc.co.uk/weather

BBC News

This is a useful site for news about droughts and other extreme weather events.

news.bbc.co.uk

UNHCR

The United Nation High Commission for Refugees website has news of all the regions struck by drought and famine at the moment.

www.unhcr.ch

Books

Awesome Forces of Nature: Dreadful Droughts
    Louise and Richard Spilsbury (Heinemann Library, 2003)
Nature on the Rampage: Droughts
    Duncan Scheff (Raintree, 2003)
Wild Weather: Drought
    Catherine Chambers (Heinemann Library, 2002)

World Wide Web

If you want to find out more about droughts, you can search the Internet using keywords like these:

- drought +news +[date you are interested in]
- drought +Sahel
- **El Niño**

Find your own keywords by using ideas from this book. Use the search tips on the next page to help you find the most useful websites.

Search tips

There are billions of pages on the Internet, so it can be difficult to find exactly what you are looking for. For example, if you just type in 'water' on a search engine like Google, you will get a list of millions of web pages. These tips will help you find useful websites more quickly:

- Decide exactly what you want to find out about first
- Use simple keywords instead of whole sentences
- Use two to six keywords in a search, putting the most important words first
- Be precise. Use names of people, places or things when you can.
- If your keywords are made up of two or more words that go together, put quote marks around them, for example "water shortage"
- Use the + sign to join keywords together, for example weather +disaster
- Adding +KS3 to your keywords may help you find web pages at the right level.

Where to search

Search engine

A search engine looks through millions of web pages and lists all the sites that match the words in the search box. They can give thousands of links, but the best matches are at the top of the list, on the first page. Try **www.bbc.co.uk**

Search directory

A search directory is more like a library of websites that have been sorted by a person instead of a computer. You can search by keyword or subject and browse through the different sites in the same way you would look through books on a library shelf. A good example is **www.yahooligans.com**

Glossary

aid organization group that helps people in need, usually in developing countries

atmosphere layer of gases that surround the Earth

barren where nothing will grow

charity organization that helps those in need

climate weather patterns over a long period of time

cloud-seeding putting chemicals into clouds to make rain

condensation droplets of water formed from water vapour when air cools

condense when a gas turns into a liquid

continent large area of land surrounded by sea

current steady flow of water or air in one direction

dam barrier built across a river or stream to stop the water flowing

developed country rich country with modern living conditions, such as Australia, Britain and the USA

developing country poor country that is trying to become richer and improve its living conditions, like Ethiopia and Somalia in Africa

diet amount and type of food eaten

disability injury or disease that prevents a person doing something

drought-resistant able to grow even in drought conditions

dust storm cloud of dust blown by the wind

El Niño pattern of wind and ocean currents that brings extreme weather

erosion wearing away by action of wind and water

evaporate change from liquid water into invisible water vapour

exhaust waste gases from a vehicle's engine

famine going without food for a long time

fertile capable of growing plants

fertility ability to grow things

fodder animal feed

forecast give information about something that might happen

germinate start to grow

global warming way that the Earth's climate is warming up

groundwater water stored beneath the soil

hydro-electric power electricity produced by running water

infrared light that is produced by heat sources

insurance agreement to provide money in case of a disaster

irrigate water crops

livestock farm animals

manure animal dung used as a fertilizer

meteorologist person who studies and reports on the weather

migration   moving from one place to settle in another

mineral salt   salts found in the soil

monitor   watch carefully

NGO   non-governmental organization, also called an aid organization

nomadic   moving from place to place

nutrient   substance needed for growth

pollution   presence of high levels of harmful substances

population   total number of people living in a place

pressure   force pressing down

priority   most important thing

rainforest   dense evergreen forest that grows in hot, rainy parts of the world

ration   share out fairly

refugee camp   place where migrating people gather to receive aid

reproduce   make offspring or members of the same species

reservoir   man-made or natural lake or large tank for storing water

satellite   object in space used to observe our planet

sewage   waste water produced by humans

standpipe   upright water pipe with a tap on it

starve   have little or no food

terrace   flat area on a hillside

topsoil   top layer of soil, often containing material from plants and animals

traditional   way of life passed down from generation to generation

transpiration   way plants lose water from their leaves through evaporation

undergrowth   plants that grow beneath trees in a forest

vegetation   all the plants that grow in an area

water source   place where water is found, such as a river, lake or well

water vapour   water in the form of an invisible gas in the air

wilt   when plants droop because of lack of water

wind break   screen to stop the wind

Index